Where Is
the Eiffel Tower?

by Dina Anastasio

illustrated by Tim Foley

Penguin Workshop

For Eliza and Isabella.
We'll always have Paris—DA

PENGUIN WORKSHOP
An Imprint of Penguin Random House LLC, New York

Visit us online at www.penguinrandomhouse.com.

Library of Congress Control Number: 2017010008

ISBN 9780451533845   10 9

Contents

Where Is the Eiffel Tower?

On March 31, 1889, Gustave Eiffel climbed 1,710 steps to the top of his new tower. He attached the striped blue, white, and red French flag to the flagpole. The flag fluttered in the wind. He looked down. The entire city of Paris, France, spread out 934 feet below him. He watched the boats moving back and forth along the Seine River that flows through the center of the city.

Across the river, on the right bank, people were strolling along the wide boulevard toward the limestone Arc de Triomphe monument. Others were relaxing on benches in the gardens near the Louvre Museum. Farther up the river, Gustave could view Notre-Dame Cathedral, one of the city's oldest stone buildings.

Next to his tower, on the river's left bank, a world's fair called the Exposition Universelle was getting ready for its May 6 opening day. Hundreds of thousands of visitors were expected. Artists and inventors would exhibit their newest creations. Merchants from all over the world would demonstrate their latest products. Gustave Eiffel's tower would be the entrance to the fair.

Gustave walked down the stairs. At the bottom, the men who had worked on the tower were waiting. So were Paris dignitaries and reporters.

Gustave thanked all the workers. It had been two years, two months, and five days since they dug the first hole. During that time, Parisians had watched Gustave's wrought-iron tower rise higher and higher. Now it was the tallest structure in the world.

Many critics called it a monstrosity. A giant, ugly smokestack.

On May 6, when the fair opened, the public would see—and decide—for themselves. It is doubtful that very many people at that time expected the Eiffel Tower to become one of the most famous landmarks anywhere on earth.

France

France is a country in western Europe. It is almost as big as Texas, but not quite.

The official language of France is French.

The capital is Paris.

France is part of the European Union. Its money is the euro.

The French flag has three equal-size vertical stripes. They are blue, white, and red. The flag is called the *tricolore*.

France is officially named the French Republic. It became a republic in 1792, after the French Revolution.

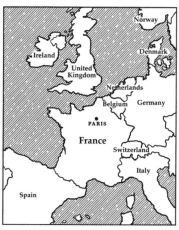

CHAPTER 1
Opening Day

The fair opened on a beautiful, cool spring day. An enormous crowd of people from France and other parts of the world waited.

Shortly after two o'clock in the afternoon, the French president pushed a button. Three fountains lit by electric lights spewed forth water from the ground beside the tower. The crowds cheered.

For more than two years, Parisians had seen this strange metal creation rise. They knew that its giant legs faced north, south, east, and west, like the points of a compass. They had read about the delicate lattice ironwork and other details. They had heard about the four restaurants that would serve wonderful food, and the observation deck at the very top.

Today was the day! Finally they would be able to examine the whole tower not only from the outside, but from the inside, too. They could ride the elevators all the way to the top . . .

Except the elevators weren't working. Even worse, the stairs weren't ready for the public. Up on the tower, workmen were still sawing and hammering. Workers were hurrying to finish painting the tower dark red. Visitors would have to wait to go inside.

The crowd was disappointed. They had been reading about the tower in newspapers. Many reporters despised it. Others praised it. A few admitted they had no idea what this iron thing was supposed to be. Many people had written letters to the editor protesting the tower. Parisians were proud of their long past. They were proud of all the magnificent old stone buildings and monuments that lined their boulevards. This tower was so different. It didn't fit in with the rest of the city.

The Arc de Triomphe

The Champs-Élysées, the main boulevard of Paris

The 1889 Paris fair was celebrating the one hundredth anniversary of the French Revolution. It had brought about the country's first democratic government. Shouldn't the fair's entrance be a monument to France's noble history?

But others disagreed. The fair was also supposed to show off everything new in art and science. Countries from all over the world were exhibiting their latest products. Shouldn't the entrance to the fair celebrate the new instead of

the old? Shouldn't visitors enter the fair through something exciting and modern?

The crowd moved past the tower. Inside the fairground, there was so much to see. People went from one pavilion to another, either on foot or by tram or rickshaw. They watched Turkish men making shoes. They saw jewelry being made in the Tunisian pavilion. They ate North African couscous and listened to Arab music as they sipped imported teas.

However, many pavilions along the lovely tree-lined paths were incomplete. In the Palace of Fine Arts building, French and American paintings had yet to be hung. Mosaics, tapestries, glasswork, and sculptures from countries around the world were still being unpacked.

Many visitors had been hoping to see the beautiful fifteen-acre Gallery of Machines. They had heard that the newest inventions and gadgets would be on exhibit. But again, fairgoers were disappointed. Most exhibits would not be ready for at least another week.

Gallery of Machines

Happily, that wasn't the case with Thomas Edison's latest invention. Edison was famous worldwide. His new electric lightbulbs glowed around the fair and shimmered in the fountains. Now visitors could examine his latest wonder—the phonograph. It could record sounds and music and play them on round wax cylinders. The phonograph was the talk of the fair.

Until then, to hear music you had to be where it was being performed. People went to concerts or played musical instruments at home. For the first time, they could listen to music and words coming from a machine. And they could try out another new idea: earphones. The idea came from watching doctors listen to the beating of human hearts. Doctors had been using in-ear listening devices attached to stethoscopes for forty years. Now they could be used to listen to music.

A machine that records sound? people asked as they waited in line. *A machine that plays music? A machine that speaks?* Truly the future had arrived!

As day turned to night, the fair glowed. Edison's electric lights meant it could stay open past dark. Earlier fairs had closed at sundown.

Later that night, as the first day of the fair came to a close, fireworks lit up the sky.

At 10:00 p.m., the dark red Eiffel Tower lit up. Green Roman candles exploded near the top. It was a glorious end to the day.

Inside the tower, however, Gustave Eiffel was filled with despair. He was fifty-six years old. To many who knew him, it seemed that he had been preparing for this moment most of his life. He had tried his best to have the tower ready before the fair opened, but he had failed. Visitors would have to wait nine more days to explore it.

Thank You, Mr. Edison

Thomas Alva Edison wanted to figure out how to record people talking. Before long, he came up with a cylinder wrapped in tinfoil that spun around and made high and low sounds when poked by a needle, called a stylus. He also thought of using round, grooved discs made of wax. His disc inventions, later called records, are still played on turntables today.

In 1891 he invented the first motion-picture camera and viewing apparatus, the Kinetoscope.

So thank you, Mr. Edison.

CHAPTER 2
Gustave Eiffel

Alexandre-Gustave Eiffel was born in Dijon, France, on December 15, 1832. Gustave was close to both of his parents. His father, Alexandre, was an artist, a reader, a thinker, and a dreamer.

His mother, Catherine, was much more practical. She was good at making plans, meeting deadlines, and handling money.

When Gustave was young, his parents ran a thriving business that transported coal from mines to places around the world. Gustave and his two younger sisters spent many happy days at the canal port in Dijon. He watched carts filled with coal arrive from the mines and get transferred to ships. He loved the hustle and bustle of boats being loaded and unloaded at all hours and in all kinds of weather.

As the coal business grew, his parents spent more and more time working. Gustave went to live with his mother's mother, who was blind. His grandmother was strict, but Gustave didn't seem to mind that much.

What Gustave didn't like was school. He found it boring and a waste of time compared to what was happening on the busy canal. He had a hard time keeping his mind on his work, so his grades were not good. He did just enough work to keep up.

When Gustave was twelve, he took his first trip to Paris. He had never been on a train before, and he loved every minute of it.

In Paris, he went to the theater and the ballet. Gustave was determined to return to the wonderful city as soon as he could.

Back at school, he found teachers that understood his curiosity and imagination. They introduced him to literature and history. He also embraced

science. His grades soared, and he was accepted at a college on the left bank of the Seine River in Paris, not far from where his tower would rise almost forty years later.

It was at college that Gustave fell in love with metal.

Paris was changing. Architects were just beginning to use metal instead of stone. Iron bridges were being built. Gustave was curious about how metal could be used. How could he bend it? How could he shape it? What could he build? There were so many possibilities. He didn't know all the answers yet. He would need to learn how to create iron structures.

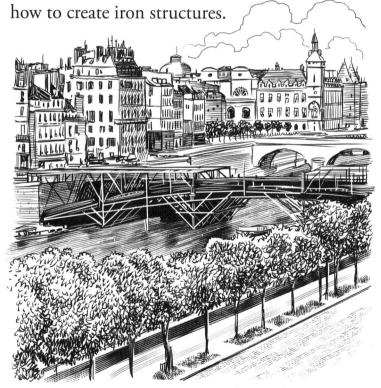

A wrought-iron bridge under construction

Gustave enrolled in engineering school. After he graduated, he worked an unpaid job in an iron foundry owned by his brother-in-law. He watched and listened.

In 1862, when Gustave was thirty years old, he married Marie Gaudelet. In need of money, he moved on to a paid job in a company that designed railway engines. He was fascinated by curving, long-distance railway tracks.

Gustave's life was changing. His family was growing. In time, the Eiffels would have three daughters and two sons. But work was Gustave's passion. He never wavered in his love for metal. He opened his own company and hired engineers, architects, and designers. Together, they went on to create bridges, railway stations, churches, and other buildings all over the world. Between 1882 and 1884, he created the Garabit Viaduct, the world's highest bridge at the time. His company became most famous, however, for creating the metal framework inside the Statue of Liberty.

The Garabit Viaduct

The Statue of Liberty

From 1879 to 1883, while the artist Frédéric-Auguste Bartholdi sculpted the outside of the Statue of Liberty, Gustave Eiffel and his team worked on the inside. The statue would need a metal skeleton that would remain strong for hundreds of years. Eiffel's intricate frame used flexible, flat pieces of lightweight iron to attach the inner iron skeleton to the outer copper skin.

The copper statue of the Roman goddess of liberty was a gift of friendship to the United States from the people of France. It would celebrate the freedom and independence Americans had won in the Revolutionary War.

On June 19, 1885, the Statue of Liberty arrived at her new home on Bedloe's Island in New York Harbor.

A cross-section of the Statue of Liberty

CHAPTER 3
Mr. Eiffel's Tower

On May 2, 1886, the French government announced a contest that excited Gustave because of what he might create out of iron.

Contestants were asked to submit a design for a tower that would be the entrance to the 1889 fair. The tower had to be three hundred meters high, which is more than nine hundred feet. That would make it the tallest structure in the world. A structure so high would show what a great country France had become in the last one hundred years. In addition, the tower must be a temporary structure that was easy to put up and take down.

Gustave wanted to enter the contest—and win!

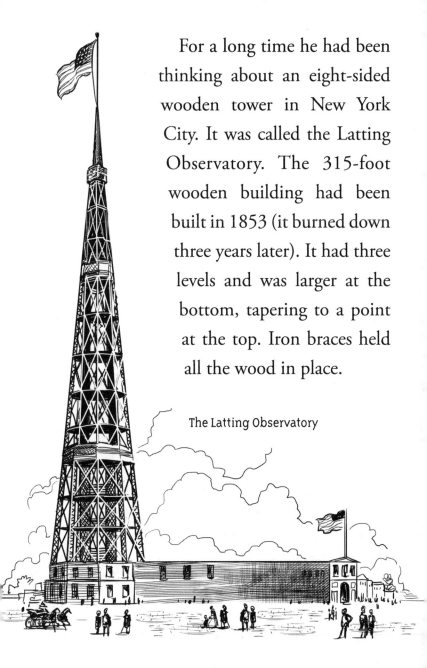

For a long time he had been thinking about an eight-sided wooden tower in New York City. It was called the Latting Observatory. The 315-foot wooden building had been built in 1853 (it burned down three years later). It had three levels and was larger at the bottom, tapering to a point at the top. Iron braces held all the wood in place.

The Latting Observatory

The wooden Latting Observatory struck Gustave as plain and unexciting. But something similar using iron would be amazing. In fact, even before the fair contest was announced, Gustave had asked Maurice Koechlin, an engineer in his drawing department, and

Maurice Koechlin

Émile Nouguier, a structural engineer, to draw plans for such a tower.

Because of the contest, Gustave worked with his top employees, redesigning the earlier drawings. The tower would be made of metal. Thousands of pieces of wrought iron

Émile Nouguier

would be used to create a perfect design. He would need rivets to hold them together. Building the tower would be like working on a huge, well-planned, perfectly designed LEGO creation.

But Gustave wanted his tower to be more than a perfectly engineered structure. His new tower would be a work of art. A modern masterpiece.

Stephen Sauvestre was Eiffel's top architect. He was also a brilliant artist. He understood Gustave's dream. Working together, the two men would create a building to be admired throughout time.

Stephen Sauvestre

Sauvestre imagined a graceful tower filled with beautiful details. His design featured swooping arches. Carved stonework would decorate the tower's legs. He suggested artistic trimmings and elegant decorations.

The judges agreed that the plan was exactly what they were looking for. Eiffel won the contest. On January 8, 1887, they signed a contract. Everyone in Gustave's company was excited.

Eiffel and his team of engineers had less than two and a half years to build the tower. They weren't worried. They had built many bridges from wrought iron. They knew how to create structures quickly and safely, ones that could withstand violent storms and allow for huge crowds.

Twenty years earlier, Eiffel had set up workshops in Levallois-Perret, a northwest suburb of Paris. It was in those buildings that most of the work on the Eiffel Tower took place.

Each piece of iron was cut, measured, numbered, and prepared to connect to the next piece. Rivet holes were drilled in each piece and precisely measured so that they would line up perfectly. Temporary pegs were used to connect the pieces. Later, when all the pieces were connected at the fairground by the river, the pegs would be replaced by strong, permanent bolts.

As the iron pieces were being cut and fitted together in the workshop, workmen were digging holes in the soil on the Champ de Mars, a large grassy park near the Seine River.

The tower's four iron legs had to be planted deep in the ground. They also had to angle inward to the first platform. The sloping legs would hold the tower steady, even in the strongest winds.

However, the workmen soon realized that the clay soil nearest the river created a problem. It was too wet. The two legs by the river might sink. Eiffel needed to find a way to make sure all four legs stood at the same level. He decided to dig the two holes in damp soil sixteen feet deeper than the other two and pour in compressed air and extra concrete. Now the four holes were all equally deep. They were filled with cement, limestone blocks, and gravel. Iron anchors and bolts were inserted, and each iron leg was attached to a concrete column.

When the foundation was complete, horse-drawn carts delivered girders, trusses, and other wrought-iron pieces from the workshops to the building site.

Base of a leg

People in the neighborhood had seen the four holes being dug. Now they could watch the actual tower rise. Small pieces of metal were riveted together into four perfectly placed iron legs. Men worked on wooden scaffolds that were made taller as the building grew.

When the legs were in place, they formed a 410-foot square. After that, it was time to build the first floor. This would be the tower's base. It would look like a table with four legs. Once the base was in place, workers could build upward from floor to floor.

Small creeper cranes pulled trolleys filled with materials up tracks inside the four slanted legs. The tracks would later be used to move elevators full of visitors upward.

Soon, horizontal wrought-iron trusses were in place on top of the legs, joining them together. Column and platform pieces were hoisted and joined.

Workers spent longer and longer hours on the tower in order to meet the deadline. Canteens were installed on higher floors so they wouldn't have to waste time climbing up and down the steps to eat their meals.

By April 1, 1888, the first floor was complete. Four and a half months later, the second floor was finished, and seven and a half months after that, on March 31, 1889, the final piece of the tower was riveted into place. Gustave and his workers had used over eighteen thousand pieces of iron and two and a half million rivets to hold everything together.

The tower was in place. It had taken two years, two months, and five days to construct the tallest structure in the world. Newspaper reporters were amazed at how fast it had gone up. They admired Gustave's precise planning and his new, faster machines, like the hydraulic jacks and creeper cranes that

had helped speed up construction.

It was dangerous work to build so high a structure. Yet not a single person died on the job. Sadly one worker climbed the tower at night when it was closed. He was showing off for his girlfriend, and he fell to his death.

CHAPTER 4
The Critics React

During the time the tower was constructed, buildings were growing taller all over the world. Big cities were running out of land. Tall buildings were the future. Wrought iron was the perfect material. It was easier to work with than stone.

The critics of the Eiffel Tower fumed. This was Paris, after all. A magnificent city built of beautiful stone.

No one protested as loudly as a group of painters, sculptors, architects, and writers. After seeing the plans for the tower, three hundred of them signed a protest against its construction. They called themselves the "Committee of Three Hundred," named for the three-hundred-meter tower. Artists who signed included the composer

Charles Gounod, the poet Paul Verlaine, the writer and playwright Alexandre Dumas Jr., and many others.

The protest was published in the *Le Temps* newspaper on February 14, 1887.

"Listen to our plea! Imagine now a ridiculous tall tower dominating Paris like a gigantic black factory smokestack."

Artists compared the tower to a streetlamp, a skeleton, and a factory pipe.

Guy de Maupassant

One of the most famous protestors was Guy de Maupassant, a writer who was well known for his short stories. He hated the tower so much that when it opened, he couldn't bear to look at it. He decided to eat his lunch in one of the tower's restaurants because that was the only place where he didn't have to look at the tower itself. He later left France, saying he wanted to get away from the Eiffel Tower. He described it as, "This high and skinny pyramid of iron ladders, this giant ungainly skeleton upon a base that looks built to carry a colossal monument of Cyclops [a one-eyed monster], but which just peters out into a ridiculous thin shape like a factory chimney."

There was also Charles Garnier, one of the most talented architects in France. Ten years earlier, Gustave and Charles had worked together on a rotating dome for an observatory in Nice, France. Gustave called it his favorite project at the

Charles Garnier

time. The two men liked each other. Now Charles was Gustave's harshest critic.

The observatory in Nice, France

Charles Garnier had designed the Paris Opera House, one of the most glorious stone buildings in the city. Completed in 1875, it was called the Palais Garnier, or the Opéra Garnier, after the man who created it. Theatergoers arriving in horse-drawn carriages were greeted

by statues and gargoyles on the outside and a world of luxury on the inside: staircases and statues made from different shades of the finest marble, and domed ceilings with gilded moldings and magnificent art.

Most Parisians considered it a lavish, glittering masterpiece.

Eiffel's simple wrought-iron tower was as different from Garnier's landmark as a candlestick from a chandelier.

Besides finding metal buildings ugly, Garnier was mad. The ridiculous tower was going to dwarf something he had designed for the fair. His Exposition of Human Habitation was located directly below the Eiffel Tower. It consisted of forty-nine different kinds of homes, from palaces to huts, to show how people around the world lived.

Exposition of Human Habitation

As Garnier continued to seethe about the tower, many other critics changed their minds. Once inside, they were able to study the artistic details of the lattice ironwork. They could stand at the top and take in the panoramic view of Paris.

They noticed how the light moved in and out of the spaces between the girders. How could they have been so wrong? they wondered. Mr. Eiffel's tower wasn't a monstrosity at all. It was a brilliant work of art!

CHAPTER 5
The Tower Is Open

On May 15, 1889, the Eiffel Tower officially opened to the public. Gustave Eiffel was the first to sign the guest book: "Ten minutes to twelve, May 15, 1889. The tower is opened to the public. At last!"

Thousands bought tickets. Gustave had paid for most of the construction himself—about $36 million in today's money. The line of ticket-buyers meant the tower would be a success. In fact, Gustave earned all his money back in less than a year.

Because of still-unfinished elevators, the crowds trudged up the iron stairs. They felt the wind blowing harder as they climbed higher. They noticed the engraved names of seventy-two

important French scientists, mathematicians, and engineers, and the names of the 199 men who had worked on the tower.

In a tiny office on the second level, *Le Figaro*, a popular newspaper, set up a printing press. Their daily newsletter would cover news from the tower. The names of visitors in the guest book would also be published in the paper.

Nearby, visitors could send messages from the new telegraph office.

Most people praised the tower, but some American visitors had mixed feelings about this new landmark. They were in awe of it, but they were also bothered. Until then, the 555-foot Washington Monument, in Washington, DC, had been the tallest structure in the world. This new iron tower was almost twice as tall.

In his office on the third level, Gustave was frustrated. He couldn't stop thinking about the elevator problem. From the very beginning, he had been in charge of every detail of the tower, but he had needed the

The Washington Monument

Otis company to build and install the elevators. There was no way around it. A one-thousand-foot building would, of course, require elevators to carry visitors to the top.

Most tall buildings include elevators that move straight up and down. But Gustave had always wanted something more unusual for his visitors. He wanted them to see and admire every one of the eighteen thousand pieces of iron in his masterpiece.

After a great deal of thought, he had decided that he needed two sets of elevators. They would look like glass cages. One set would move straight up two of the legs to the first level. The second set of elevators would travel on a curve up the other two legs from the ground to the second, much higher level. At this point, visitors would then have to change to a final elevator that would carry them the rest of the way.

Now the elevators had finally been installed, but the safety tests hadn't been performed. Gustave

wondered if anyone would ever be able to ride to the top of his beloved creation.

At last, two weeks after the Eiffel Tower's official opening, a test was done on the elevators' safety brakes. What would happen if the cables broke? Would the safety brakes stop the elevators from falling? Would the elevators' glass walls shatter?

Representatives from the Otis Elevator Company had sailed from America to join Gustave for the test. Reporters gathered to watch.

A rope replaced the steel cable. The elevator was filled with lead instead of people. It was time. Everyone waited.

A carpenter raised his hatchet. He cut the rope. The elevator dropped. It swung back and forth. It jerked. It stopped.

The safety brakes held. The elevator had passed its final test. It was ready for visitors.

Finally, in June, the five hydraulic elevators were moving up and down the tower.

As the elevators rose, visitors could look out through the top halves made of glass. They could see Gustave Eiffel's office, where he welcomed visitors.

Three months later, Thomas Edison paid him a visit. He brought a gift, one of the first phonographs ever used in Europe. It is still in Gustave Eiffel's office to this day.

At the top, visitors could send letters and postcards from a small post office. They could see a blue, white, and red beacon light that moved across the sky. A cannon that boomed at the beginning and end of the fair each day was up there, too.

The view of Paris was spectacular. Few people had ever seen land from such a height. Some balloonists had risen higher. Some people had climbed taller mountains. But there were no airplanes, so no one had flown. Visitors were amazed as they looked down. Everything on the ground seemed so small.

Gustave had always been interested in weather. So shortly after the tower opened, he installed a small weather station at the top. From there, he was able to measure temperature, wind speed, rain, and snow. The day's weather was announced in *Le Figaro*'s daily tower newspaper.

Now that his tower was finished, Gustave could sit in his office and think about what he had accomplished. The fair below was up and running. He had created the perfect entrance. He felt proud.

CHAPTER 6
The Fair Below

Down below, most of the exhibitions were finally up and running. More than 61,000 exhibitors displayed products and artwork, and performed music, dance, and theater. Although they came from all over the world, more than half of the exhibitors were from France or French colonies.

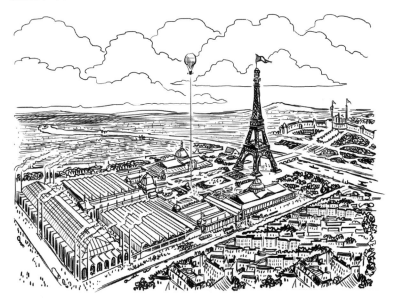

French Colonies

A colony is a country or area that is ruled by another country, usually one that is bigger and far away. America was one of Great Britain's colonies until the colonists fought the Revolutionary War and won their freedom.

France's colonies in 1889

In 1889, France controlled many distant countries. Each was very different and had its own culture. This fair was their chance to show the world how they ate, dressed, and lived.

The French colonial expositions were located in the Esplanade des Invalides, up the river from the Eiffel Tower. Visitors were given a ticket called the "magic carpet" that allowed them to experience cultures from all over the world.

Actors from Indochina, now called Vietnam, put on a show. Dancers from Java performed native dances. Workers and performers lived in

villages with houses like the ones in distant Tahiti and Senegal.

But the 1889 fair was not just about the French and their colonies. Beautiful tiles adorned a Tunisian palace. Algerians were at work, embroidering slippers and weaving baskets. Egyptian donkeys pulled carts. There was even a working English dairy where cows gave fresh milk. Visitors could watch Devonshire cream being made and eat delicious homemade ice cream at small tables.

One of the most admired exhibitions was a huge model of the earth, accurately scaled to size. With a diameter of forty-two feet, it was exactly one-millionth the size of the earth. Like the fair itself, this rotating globe was meant to introduce visitors to the world as a whole. Perfectly measured countries, cities, bodies of water, mountains, shipping routes, telegraph lines, and a variety of geographical facts were painted on the outside.

Visitors were especially excited to see the American exhibits. Thomas Edison's electric lights glittered everywhere. Otis elevators carried passengers to the top of the Eiffel Tower. Now visitors could learn about American culture as well. They could view the newest art from the 255 American painters exhibiting at the fair. Many were especially excited to see the much-talked-about portraits by John Singer Sargent, who would win a medal of honor at the medal ceremony on September 29.

And everyone wanted to try out the telephone display! Alexander Graham Bell had invented the telephone thirteen years earlier, but long-distance calling was still in the future. People wondered what it would sound like. Inside the exhibit, visitors found a line of telephones on one wall.

Miles away, at the Paris Opera House, telephone receivers were broadcasting live music. The concert could be heard through the phones, all the way across the city. It was incredible!

But everyone, it seemed, couldn't wait to see Thomas Edison's newest inventions. His exhibit was inside the beautiful fifteen-acre glass-and-steel Gallery of Machines. Hurrying into the gallery, visitors were surrounded by electric lights that blinked, buzzed, and fizzled. Pumps shuddered and thumped. Engines pounded and clanked.

Some people stopped to inspect the new machines, but most rushed to try out Edison's phonograph. Earphones were passed from visitor to visitor. Each person was allowed three minutes to listen to the national anthems of France and the United States.

But America didn't just bring inventions and art. They also brought Buffalo Bill and Annie Oakley. On the other side of the river, beyond the Louvre Museum, Buffalo Bill Cody was putting on his very popular Wild West show.

During the 1800s, Americans had been moving west. Before the first cross-country railroad was completed in 1869, pioneers traveled in covered wagons. Many American Indian tribes hunted buffalo. Mail was delivered by the Pony Express, on horseback or in wagons. The western plains were wild and dangerous.

In a Paris amphitheater, Buffalo Bill's touring show re-created the Wild West—or at least the Wild West as white Americans liked to picture it.

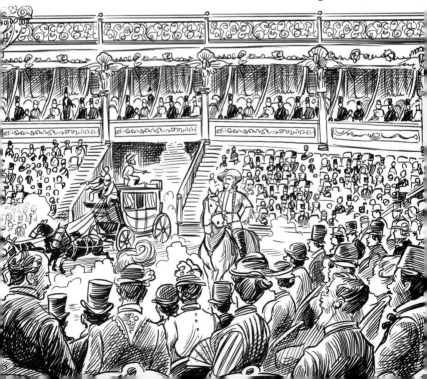

Plains Indians riding bareback did battle with Pony Express messengers. Led by Buffalo Bill, cowboys on horseback shouted and raised their rifles as they raced to save the passengers on the wagon train. Annie Oakley, the show's world-famous five-foot-tall sharpshooter, demonstrated why she was known as "Little Sure Shot." She was able to shoot a cigar out of her husband's mouth!

That night, as visitors on both sides of the Seine left the fairground, they stopped and looked up. The tower was blazing with light. The spotlight was spinning colors through the sky. The fountains below it were dancing.

In September, officials agreed to keep the fair open for an extra week. It would close exactly three months after it opened. The 1889 Exposition Universelle had been a huge success.

CHAPTER 7
What Can You Do with a Tower?

Paris officials wanted to take down the tower when the fair closed. That had been the plan from the start. The city owned the land it was built on, and the city wanted it back. Gustave, on the other hand, hoped the tower would stand forever.

An agreement was finally signed. His tower could remain where it was until 1909. That was better, but not good enough for Gustave. He now had twenty years to figure out how to make the tower a permanent landmark, one that would stand for hundreds of years.

Gustave soon came up with a plan. At that time, people used telegraphs to send messages long distances over land. At sea, ships in trouble used Morse code. Messages were carried through wires and cables under the ocean.

But something new was happening. An inventor named Guglielmo Marconi was working on a way to send messages long distances through the air on radio waves. His invention did not use wires. Messages would be transmitted and received using an antenna.

Wireless radio waves fascinated Gustave. He had been using his tower to conduct weather experiments. Why not use it to experiment with radio waves?

Gustave worked hard. He brought in an inventor named Eugène Ducretet to help. They raised an antenna above the third floor. Finally, on November 5, 1898, a signal was sent from the tower and picked up at the Panthéon, about three miles away. Still, Paris officials insisted the tower had to be taken down in 1909.

Gustave was desperate. How could he convince

the officials to let his tower stand? Hadn't they been impressed with his radio work?

Then Gustave had a brainstorm. Wasn't the French military doing wireless experiments? Didn't it need a better way to transmit and receive messages?

Gustave went to the military. Okay, the officials said. They'd agree to try using the tower for some of their experiments. The military installed better and higher antennas. It worked. They could send clearer messages and orders to more distant soldiers and sailors.

The military was convinced. Now Gustave had to convince the Paris officials. It took time, but eventually, on January 1, 1910, an agreement to save the Eiffel Tower was signed.

Over the years, new ways to use radio waves were discovered. More advanced wireless devices were invented. By 1920, a machine called the radio could broadcast programs that people listened to from far away. In the mid-twentieth century, television began broadcasting programs that people could see as well as hear. The tower was becoming more and more important. Higher antennas were added to help send and receive signals.

Today, 120 antennas at the top of the Eiffel Tower help send messages to the farthest points of the globe.

Guglielmo Marconi (1874–1937)

Guglielmo Marconi was born in Bologna, Italy, on April 25, 1874. When he was a boy, he was fascinated by science. As he grew older, he became interested in the way people sent and received messages and signals over long distances. At the time, information was transmitted over wires and cables.

Marconi had a better idea. Maybe it was possible to send signals through the air using electromagnetic radiation. He created equipment that produced radio waves. Then he conducted experiments. Before long, he was able to send signals, first one mile, then twelve miles.

Marconi wondered how far his signals could go. Could a wireless signal be sent from England to Newfoundland, Canada? It was 2,100 miles, all the way across the Atlantic Ocean. Many people thought it was impossible. But Marconi decided to try.

On December 12, 1901, he succeeded. No wires or cables were used. Wireless was born.

In September 1914, Europe was fighting World War I. German troops had taken over Belgium. They were fighting to capture France. As the Germans moved closer to Paris, French soldiers fought one of the most important battles of the war. It took place at the Marne River, thirty miles from Paris.

The tower was closed to the public during the war, but the antennas continued to be used. As the battle raged on, messages to French troops were being transmitted from the top of the tower.

Also, the tower's transmitters were able to pick up German messages. This helped the French soldiers know what the enemy was up to. The Battle of the Marne lasted about a week. When it was over, the Germans retreated. Paris was safe. In 1918, Germany surrendered, ending World War I.

A little more than twenty years later, Germany again went to war against many countries in Europe, including France. In 1940, German Nazi soldiers moved into the center of Paris to occupy the city. It was a terrible time for France.

At the Eiffel Tower, a French fireman was forced to take down the national flag of France. The Nazis then raised their own flag.

However, by 1944, Adolf Hitler, the Nazi leader, could see that Germany was losing the war. So he called in General Dietrich von Choltitz. He was the German commander and governor of occupied Paris. Hitler gave him an order: Before Paris was free again, von Choltitz must reduce the city to rubble. No famous building or monument could be left standing. Notre-Dame Cathedral, the Louvre Museum,

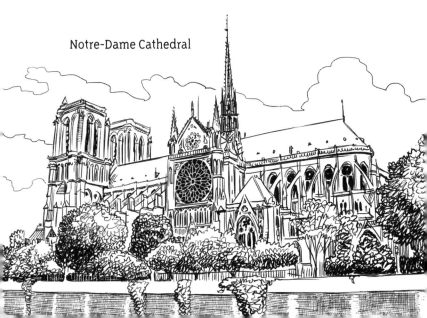

Notre-Dame Cathedral

the Arc de Triomphe, the Eiffel Tower, and other beloved Parisian landmarks must be blown up. Under no circumstances should von Choltitz leave Paris without destroying it.

The battle to free Paris from the Germans began in August 1944. The Allied troops (Americans and British) were moving closer and closer to Paris. Soon they would arrive and liberate the city. Hitler ordered that explosives be put in place around Paris—on bridges, buildings, and monuments. Von Choltitz followed these orders. But he did not obey Hitler's final command. He never pushed the buttons that would have fired the explosives.

On August 24, French and American troops moved into Paris. Parisians took up guns and rushed into the streets to help win back their city. The Germans surrendered on August 25, 1944.

Von Choltitz had plenty of time and

opportunity to destroy Paris. Why, instead, did he save the city? His reasons are still unclear.

There are many different theories. Von Choltitz himself stated, "If for the first time I had disobeyed, it was because I knew that Hitler was insane." His son maintained his father understood there was no reason to take down the buildings and chose to save the city.

French people found that impossible to believe. Von Choltitz had killed many Parisians; he had no love for their city. So perhaps somewhere in Paris, a Parisian stopped von Choltitz from that horrible act.

With Paris now freed, the moment had come to pull down the hated Nazi flag from the Eiffel Tower. The same man who had removed the French flag in 1940 was chosen to put up the *tricolore* of blue, white, and red. But all French flags had been destroyed by the Nazis during the war. So he ended up making a three-color flag out of sheets, then climbed to the top of the tower and raised the giant banner.

The Eiffel Tower stood proud once more, truly a symbol of France's liberty.

CHAPTER 8
Can You Imagine?

Ever since the tower opened, people have looked up and thought about possibilities. Some were silly. Some were profound.

How fast can I run to the top? Is it possible to ride down on a bicycle? How would it feel to parachute off something so high? Can I make it all the way up the iron girders? Should I climb this way? That way? How would it feel to fly around or under it? And most important: If Gustave Eiffel could create something like this, then what can I do?

Sylvain Dornon, a French baker, climbed his way to fame. On September 9, 1891, he worked his way up 347 steps to the tower's first level on stilts.

In 1901, a man named Alberto Santos-Dumont decided to become the first person to fly all the way around the tower. Planes had not yet been invented. It would be two years before Orville and Wilbur Wright's first powered flight. Santos-Dumont flew in a hot-air balloon and won a prize of one hundred thousand French francs from a rich businessman.

As time passed, the stunts grew more dangerous. Too many failed, so laws were made. No jumping allowed! No flying near the tower! No climbing the metal pieces!

Did that stop the daredevils?

No!

In 1912, a tailor designed and created a thick parachute suit that he hoped would save pilots if

they fell or jumped from planes. He climbed the tower and jumped. It didn't work, and he died.

In 1923, a Paris journalist rode his bike down the tower staircase. He survived and was arrested at the bottom.

As aviation advanced, several pilots flew small planes between the tower's legs.

In 1987, a man from New Zealand bungee-jumped from the second floor.

But perhaps the most famous daredevil of all was Philippe Petit, a world-class tightrope walker. On August 26, 1989, Petit stretched a 2,300-foot cable from the right bank of the Seine River to the second level of the Eiffel Tower on the left bank.

Philippe had been invited to perform his act

by French president Jacques Chirac to celebrate the two hundredth anniversary of the French Republic. As thousands of spectators on both sides of the river watched, he walked up the cable. He was dressed in a red, green, and yellow skintight suit. He carried a long pole to balance himself. At the end of his walk, as he stepped onto the tower, he was greeted by President Chirac.

Philippe Petit (1949–)

Philippe Petit was born in France on August 13, 1949. Growing up, he loved climbing. When he was

sixteen, he rigged up a rope between two trees and taught himself to walk across it. He practiced. Then he practiced some more. He studied weather, wind, distance, measurements, rigging, and timing.

At 7:00 a.m. on August 7, 1974, Philippe walked a wire between the World Trade Center's twin towers in New York City. He was 1,368 feet—one-quarter of a mile—above the sidewalks below. Without a net.

This was the walk that made him world famous. He was twenty-four years old. Every detail had been considered. He had studied the architecture and the way the wind swayed the towers. He had taken

photographs and made drawings. Using a bow and arrow, he had worked out a way to rig the cable from tower to tower, a 138-foot space.

Petit kneeled, danced, lay on the wire, and walked back and forth eight times for forty-five minutes. He was arrested for trespassing and disorderly conduct. Many people who had seen his act protested his arrest. He was released on the condition that he entertain children in New York City's Central Park.

Since then, Philippe Petit has performed all over the world, at churches, circuses, operas, museums, railway stations, and the Eiffel Tower.

CHAPTER 9
The Tower Today

Gustave Eiffel's tower still stands proudly beside the Seine River. His dream to create a structure that would remain forever has come true. It is considered one of the most important landmarks in Paris and one of the world's greatest buildings.

Gustave died at his home in Paris on December 27, 1923. He was listening to a recording of Beethoven's Symphony No. 5. He was ninety-one years old. Much of his long life was spent in his tower. He conducted experiments with metal, wind, flight, weather, and radio waves, and he checked to make sure that all was well with his most beloved building.

The Eiffel Tower is no longer the tallest

structure in the world. In 1930, the Chrysler Building in New York City took over that record. Even taller buildings followed. But few structures can match Gustave Eiffel's wrought-iron masterpiece for creativity.

The Chrysler Building

Night after night, the "Iron Lady," as the tower is often called, continues to shine in Paris. Almost seven million people visit each year, more than any other monument in the world. Three out of four come from countries other than France. Some climb the steps all the way to the top. Others ride the glass elevators. A few call the tower ugly, but most disagree. They use words like *original, unusual, brilliant, elegant, a dancing wonder, a magical masterpiece.*

The Eiffel Tower is not exactly the same as it was in 1889. The elevators are faster and more efficient. There are more shops and restaurants. The tower is no longer red. Painters use a bronze color now.

By 1981, the tower was in need of a major reconstruction. It was almost one hundred years old. Newer and heavier equipment, restaurants, shops, and antennas had been added over the years. The excess weight was causing problems.

The tower was made one hundred tons lighter. Many of the earlier, heavy ornaments and decorations were removed. New, lighter materials were used.

Elevators and staircases were updated. Security measures were installed.

In 2014, a new, lighter, illuminated glass first floor was added. It is a big hit with visitors.

Gustave Eiffel's original office has been restored. Visitors can see wax models of Gustave and Thomas Edison along with the phonograph that Edison brought as a gift.

Visitors can choose between fine dining restaurants, bars, or buffets serving snacks and

sandwiches. They can buy postcards and other souvenirs in the shops. In winter, visitors can even skate on a temporary rink.

What makes the Eiffel Tower so exciting has not changed. From the top, people still look down in wonder on the beautiful city of Paris.

The lit-up tower can still be seen from all over the city. In 1889, hundreds of gas lamps made it shine. Today, twenty thousand lightbulbs twinkle for five minutes every hour on the hour each night.

On special occasions, lights are coordinated with music, and the tower seems to be dancing.

At times, the whole tower shines blue, white, and red: the colors of the French flag.

It has been more than 130 years since Gustave first attached a French flag to the top of his newly opened creation. It was supposed to be torn down twenty years later. But it is still there today, standing tall, welcoming visitors from all over the world.

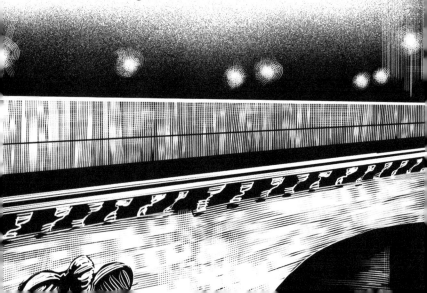

Four Towers

The Leaning Tower of Pisa

The Leaning Tower of Pisa, in Pisa, Italy, is the most famous tilting tower in the world. Construction began in 1173. Almost immediately, it began to tilt. Unlike the Eiffel Tower, the damp soil on one side was not reinforced. By 1990, it was tilting at a five-and-a-half-degree angle. Cables were attached and the ground was reinforced. The tower now leans at an angle of about four degrees.

The Space Needle

The 605-foot-tall Space Needle is an observation tower in Seattle, Washington. Built for the 1962 World's Fair, it was once the tallest building west of the Mississippi River.

The Shanghai Tower

Completed in 2015, this 2,073-foot skyscraper in Shanghai, China, is the tallest building in China, and the second tallest in the world. Its spiraling, twisting curves are better able to withstand strong winds.

The Burj Khalifa

The Burj Khalifa is a 2,722-foot skyscraper in Dubai, United Arab Emirates. Completed in 2009, it is currently the tallest structure in the world.

Timeline of the Eiffel Tower

1832	Alexandre-Gustave Eiffel born in Dijon, France
1884	Eiffel completes internal skeleton for the Statue of Liberty
1886	Contest announced to create tower entrance to 1889 Exposition Universelle
1887	Eiffel wins contest and construction of tower begins
1889	Exposition Universelle in Paris opens; Eiffel Tower opens to the public
1898	First radio transmission is sent from the tower
1905	First stair-climbing contest is held on the tower
1908	French military uses the tower to send and receive radio messages
1910	Paris officials sign contract allowing the tower to remain permanently
1915-1918	Tower closed during World War I
1921	First live radio program broadcast from the tower
1923	Eiffel dies
1936	Television antenna installed on top of tower
1940-1945	Tower closed for World War II
1952	First television program broadcast from the tower
1981-1982	Renovations made to the tower
1989	Philippe Petit walks on a wire across the Seine to second level of tower
2014	Transparent first floor added to the tower

Timeline of the World

1826 —	First photograph taken by Joseph Nicéphore Niépce
1837 —	Victoria becomes queen of the United Kingdom of Great Britain and Ireland
1861 —	American Civil War begins
1866 —	Alfred Nobel invents dynamite
1873 —	Jules Verne publishes *Around the World in Eighty Days*
1879 —	Thomas Alva Edison invents practical electric light
1896 —	First modern Olympic Games held in Athens, Greece
1898 —	Marie and Pierre Curie discover radium and polonium
1903 —	Henry Ford organizes the Ford Motor Company
1909 —	American explorers Peary and Henson reach the North Pole
1912 —	Ocean liner *Titanic* hits an iceberg and sinks
1928 —	Alexander Fleming discovers penicillin
1931 —	Empire State Building completed in New York City
1933 —	Hitler appointed chancellor of Germany
1954 —	First atomic submarine, the USS *Nautilus*, is launched
1959 —	Fidel Castro takes over Cuba
1974 —	US president Richard Nixon resigns
2009 —	Burj Khalifa in Dubai becomes the tallest structure in the world

Bibliography

*Books for young readers

*Blumenson, Martin. *Liberation*. Alexandria, VA: Time Life Books, 1978.

Collins, Larry, and Dominique Lapierre. *Is Paris Burning?* New York: Grand Central Publishing, 1994.

*Frith, Margaret. *Who Was Thomas Alva Edison?* New York: Grosset & Dunlap, 2005.

*Goldsmith, Mike. *Guglielmo Marconi* **(Scientists Who Made History)**. London: Hodder Children's Books, 2003.

Harvey, David I. *Eiffel: The Genius Who Reinvented Himself*. Stroud, Gloucestershire, UK: Sutton, 2004.

*Holub, Joan. *What Is the Statue of Liberty?* New York: Grosset & Dunlap, 2014.

Jonnes, Jill. *Eiffel's Tower: The Thrilling Story Behind Paris's Beloved Monument and the Extraordinary World's Fair That Introduced It*. New York: Penguin Books, 2010.

Lichtenstein, Grace. "Stuntman, Eluding Guards, Walks a Tightrope Between Trade Center Towers." *New York Times*, August 8, 1974.

Petit, Philippe. "Philippe Petit walks a tightrope between Manhattan's Twin Towers, 7 August 1974." *Guardian*. November 20, 2015, http://www.theguardian.com/artanddesign/2015/nov/20/philippe-petit-twin-towers-tightrope.

"Reports of the United States Commissioners to the Universal Exposition of 1889 at Paris," U.S. Government Printing Office, 1891. https://archive.org/details/cu31924107177093.

Rosbottom, Ronald C. *When Paris Went Dark: The City of Light Under German Occupation*, 1940-1944. New York: Little, Brown and Company, 2014.

Websites

The Eiffel Tower: Official Website
www.toureiffel.paris
Revolution: The Paris Exposition Universelle, 1889
www.arthurchandler.com/paris-1889-exposition/